The Library of Congress

by Andrew Santella

Content Adviser: W. Ralph Eubanks,
Director of Publishing,
The Library of Congress

Reading Adviser: Rosemary G. Palmer, Ph.D.,
Department of Literacy, College of Education,
Boise State University

COMPASS POINT BOOKS
MINNEAPOLIS, MINNESOTA

Compass Point Books
3109 West 50th Street, #115
Minneapolis, MN 55410

Visit Compass Point Books on the Internet at *www.compasspointbooks.com*
or e-mail your request to *custserv@compasspointbooks.com*

On the cover: The Library of Congress' Jefferson Building in the late 1890s

Photographs ©: Library of Congress, cover, back cover, 7, 19, 21, 22 (all), 23, 24, 25, 27, 28, 29, 37; Prints Old & Rare, back cover (far left); North Wind Picture Archives, 4; MPI/Getty Images, 9, 15; Mansell/Time Life Pictures/Getty Images, 10; Library of Congress/Time Life Pictures/Getty Images, 11; Burstein Collection/Corbis, 12; North Wind Picture Archives, 14, 17; Rare Book and Special Collections Division, Library of Congress, 16; The Granger Collection, New York, 18; Réunion des Musées Nationaux/Art Resource, N.Y., 30; PictureNet/Corbis, 31; Rare Book and Special Collections Division, Library of Congress, photograph by Roger Foley, 33; Bernard Hoffman/Time Life Pictures/Getty Images, 34, 35, 39; Corbis, 36; Sam Kittner, 40.

Editor: Julie Gassman
Page Production: James Mackey
Photo Researchers: Bobbie Nuytten and Svetlana Zhurkin
Cartographer: XNR Productions, Inc.
Library Consultant: Kathleen Baxter

Creative Director: Keith Griffin
Editorial Director: Carol Jones
Managing Editor: Catherine Neitge

Library of Congress Cataloging-in-Publication Data
Santella, Andrew.
　The Library of Congress / by Andrew Santella.
　　p. cm.— (We the people)
　Includes bibliographical references and index.
　ISBN 0-7565-1631-5
　1. Library of Congress—Juvenile literature. 2. National libraries
—Washington (D.C.)—Juvenile literature. I. Title. II. Series: We
the people (Series) (Compass Point Books)
　Z733.U6S32 2006
　027.573—dc22　　　　　　　　　　　　　　2005025083

TABLE OF CONTENTS

BOOKS ACROSS AN OCEAN

One day in 1800, a ship named *American* began its slow journey across the Atlantic Ocean. It was bound from Great Britain to the United States, a trip that would take about two weeks. Deep below its decks were 12 heavy trunks filled with books and covered with animal hides. In all, 740 volumes were packed away in the trunks—books on history, law, science, and the natural world, plus a handful of maps.

The 12 trunks were headed for Washington, D.C., the new capital of the United States. There, the books and maps would form the beginnings of a new library. No one knew it at the time, but that library would become one of the greatest the world has ever seen.

We know it today as the Library of Congress. It was founded in 1800 as a research library for members of Congress. Since then, it has grown to become what is often called the national library of the United States—reaching

The Library of Congress' main hallway and grand stairway in the 1890s

far beyond Washington. Like any public or school library, it is a resource of books, music, movies, and newspapers for people wanting to expand their knowledge. It loans books and other materials to smaller libraries across the United States. And more and more of its impressive collection can be viewed on the Internet.

The Library of Congress is home to about 29 million books stored on more than 530 miles (848 kilometers) of bookshelves. It offers more than 4 million maps, more than 2 million sound recordings, and about 12 million photographs. Its collections are spread across three large buildings on Capitol Hill.

It is home to many unique treasures. There are ancient clay tablets that tell stories of long-lost civilizations. There are famous art pieces and the most complete collection of television program recordings anywhere. There are letters written by Christopher Columbus and maps used by other great explorers in history. Some of the most important and valuable books ever published can be found there.

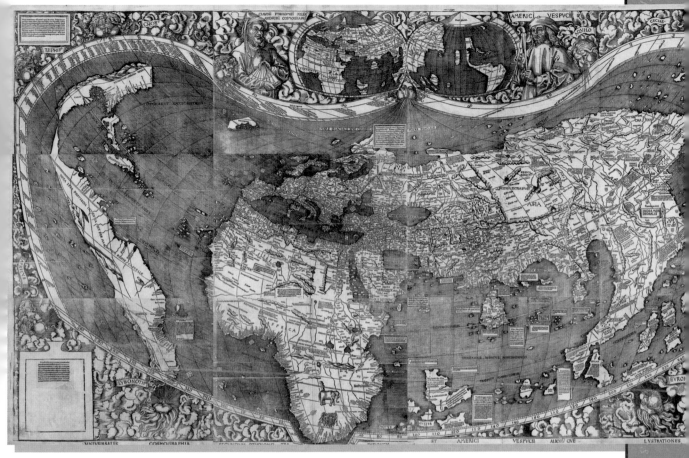

The Library of Congress is home to the first document known to name America, a map from the early 1500s.

The Library of Congress is the world's largest library and unlike any other library in the world. Each year, more than 1 million people visit it, and people from all over the globe use it. What began as a small shipment of books

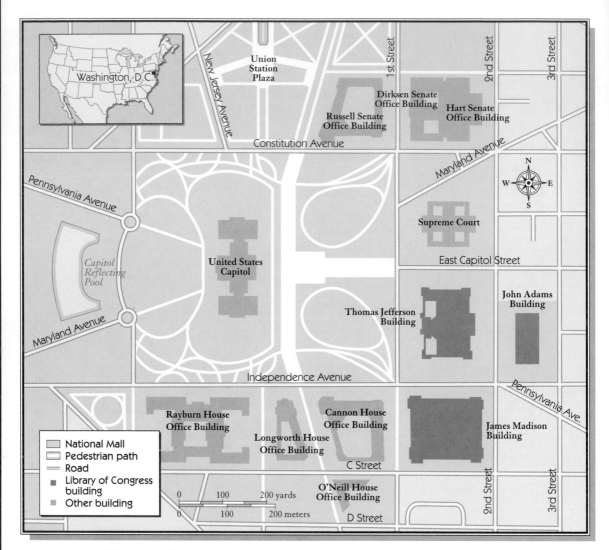

The three Library of Congress buildings are located close to the House office buildings.

brought from Europe across the Atlantic Ocean to America more than 200 years ago is today a great storehouse of knowledge and creativity.

TO SERVE CONGRESS

The United States Congress has always depended upon books. When the first Congress met in 1789, members soon sought to borrow books. It was Congress' job to create the laws that would govern the young United States. To do that, members of Congress needed to consult books on subjects like history and law. Since Congress was meeting in New York City, members borrowed books from the New York Society Library.

Later, when Congress moved to Philadelphia, it made use of the Philadelphia Library's collection. Philadelphia and New York offered excellent

An illustration of the Philadelphia Library from the 1790s

Washington, D.C., in the early 1800s

libraries, but some members of Congress believed Congress should build its own library. Nothing was done about establishing a library until 1800, when the national government moved to Washington, D.C.

At that time, the nation's capital was just a small village, with little more than a few muddy streets and some simple hotels. Even government buildings like the

Capitol had not yet been finished. There certainly were
no fine libraries like the ones found in New York and
Philadelphia. In 1800, Congress approved "the purchase of
such books as may be necessary for the use of congress at
the said city of Washington, and for fitting up a suitable
apartment for containing them." It set aside $5,000 to
establish the new library, and President John Adams signed
the bill into law. The Library of Congress was born.

To begin building the library, Congress placed an
order with a bookseller in London, England. The Library
Committee of
Congress ordered
740 books and three
maps. A room in the
north wing of the
Capitol was set aside
to store the books.
After the long trip
across the ocean, they

The U.S. Capitol as it appeared when the Library of Congress was established

11

arrived in the United States in early 1801. The secretary
of the Senate received the delivery. Relieved that they had
not been damaged by the ocean voyage, he wrote that the
books arrived "perfectly dry."

Members of Congress
realized that they would
have to set rules to
govern the use of
the library. In 1802,
President Thomas
Jefferson signed "An
Act Concerning
the Library for the
Use of Both Houses
of Congress." The
new law stated that the
library would be regu-
lated by the president of the
Senate and the speaker of the

President Thomas Jefferson

12

House of Representatives. A joint committee of Congress, with members from each house, would oversee the library. The committee was to be made up of three members from the House of Representatives and three members from the Senate. Only the U.S. president, vice president, and members of Congress would be allowed to borrow books. The daily operations of the library would be managed by a librarian appointed by the president with the approval of the Senate. The first librarian was John James Beckley, a friend of Jefferson's.

American writers, scholars, and scientists helped build the library's collection by sending copies of their writings to the library. Within 10 years, the library owned more than 3,000 books. While he was president, Jefferson took an active interest in the library. He even made a list of books that he believed the librarian should purchase.

But disaster soon struck the Library of Congress. In 1812, the United States went to war against Great Britain. Two years later, a British force sailed up Chesapeake Bay

British soldiers deliberately burned the library's books during their attack.

to invade Washington, D.C. After the British defeated
an American force outside Washington, nothing stood
between the British and the capital city. Government
officials and residents began fleeing the city. When the
British arrived, they set fire to government buildings,
including the Capitol and the Executive Mansion (later
called the White House). The Library of Congress burned
with the rest of the Capitol, and the entire library collection
was destroyed.

Even before the war ended in 1815, Congress
began considering ways to rebuild the library. Thomas

Jefferson stepped forward to provide a solution. Now living in retirement at his home, he owned one of the most impressive book collections in the country, with more than 6,000 volumes. Jefferson also badly needed money. He had acquired a large debt, having spent a great amount of money on things like extravagant parties, additions to his home, and, of course, expensive books.

Jefferson proposed selling his personal library to Congress. Congress accepted the offer and bought his collection of 6,487 books for $23,950. It took 10 wagons to transport the books to Washington, where they formed the foundation for the new Library of Congress.

These books were among those Jefferson sold to the library.

15

THE LIBRARY GROWS

The job of rebuilding the library fell to George Watterston, the third librarian of Congress. Watterston believed that the library should be more than just a reading room for Congress. He wanted it to be a national library that would reach out to the entire country. He hoped the library would one day equal the national libraries of Great Britain and France.

George Watterston

In 1824, Watterston and the library moved into a large and elegant new room in the remodeled Capitol building. He began improving and expanding the library's collection. He asked writers and artists to send copies of their work to the library.

16

The Law Library gave lawmakers and Supreme Court
justices easy access to countless legal texts.

The library continued to grow under the librarians that followed Watterston. In 1832, Congress established the Law Library of Congress to serve the Supreme Court, in addition to Congress. This library was housed within the Library of Congress and devoted to law books and legal resources from the United States, as well as other countries.

A second fire struck the Library of Congress in 1851. This fire was an accident, the result of a faulty fireplace. Still, it was just as costly as the fire set by the British in

1814. Two-thirds of the library's books were destroyed, including most of the books Thomas Jefferson had sold to the library.

The Library of Congress had to be rebuilt yet again. Not surprisingly, Congress turned to special fire prevention

The new library room opened August 23, 1853.

methods to protect the library. A new library room was built in the Capitol, using fireproof iron. Opened in 1853, it was said to be the largest room made of iron in the world. British scientist Sir Charles Lyell visited and called the elegantly decorated library "the most beautiful room in the world."

The library grew rapidly in the last decades of the 1800s, thanks to the efforts of librarian Ainsworth Rand Spofford. He served as librarian from 1864 to 1897, and he helped to greatly expand the library's collections. "I fought to bring us oceans of books and rivers of information," he said.

He arranged for the purchase of hundreds of

Ainsworth Rand Spofford

thousands of books. To do so, he had to convince members of Congress that the book collection was worth the money. He pointed out that Great Britain and other countries spent huge sums on their national libraries. He asked Congress: Shouldn't the United States do at least as much?

Spofford also convinced Congress to rewrite the nation's copyright law. Copyright is the right to publish or sell a book, song, or other work. It protects artists and authors from theft of their creations. In 1870, Congress passed the Copyright Act, which put the Library of Congress in charge of registering copyrights. The Copyright Act required anyone seeking a copyright to send two copies of their work or creation to the Library of Congress.

As a result, the library's collection grew with amazing speed. More than 11,000 books poured into the library during the first year of the Copyright Act. This rapid growth quickly turned the library into one of the largest and most extraordinary in the world.

But the growth also caused problems. There simply wasn't enough room to store all these new books. Spofford urged Congress to move the library out of its cramped quarters in the Capitol. He insisted the library needed and deserved its own building. To remind members of Congress of the problem, Spofford began piling books in

The library's collection grew so large that books and other materials had to be piled throughout the reading room and other areas of the Capitol.

21

the halls of the Capitol. Congress got the message. In 1886, it approved the construction of a new building for the Library of Congress.

A pair of photos, shot from different angles, shows the progress of construction on the new Library of Congress building over the course of one year.

A NATIONAL LIBRARY

The new Library of Congress building opened its doors in 1897. For the first time, the general public was invited to use the library's reading rooms and collections. Visitors discovered that the new building was more than just a warehouse for books. It was a showplace for the art and culture of the United States and the world.

The huge building covered an entire city block. Its Great Hall measured 75 feet (22.8 meters) high from floor to

The rotunda in the main reading room is one of the library's most stunning features.

*A painting, part of a five-panel mural titled "Government,"
is in the Thomas Jefferson Building.*

ceiling. The dome atop the library was covered in gold
leaf. Inside, visitors were dazzled by sculptures, mosaics,
murals, and paintings. More than 50 American artists
contributed work to the library. The grand new building
announced to the world that the Library of Congress was a
national treasure. Today, that building is called the Thomas

Jefferson Building. It is one of three Library of Congress buildings on Capitol Hill.

In the early 1900s, the Library of Congress took the lead in introducing new ways of serving readers and researchers. One was a method of organizing books, created by Librarian of Congress Herbert Putnam. The method was later named the Library of Congress Classification System, and it is still in use today.

To ensure that books can be easily found, libraries need

Herbert Putnam in his office

25

a system for keeping them in order. For years, the library had used a system devised by Thomas Jefferson that divided volumes into three areas: memory, reason, and imagination. But Putnam's new system divided all knowledge into 20 categories, each identified by a specific letter. Each book in the library is given a series of letters and numbers that indicate which category it best fits. Then it is stored on shelves with other books in the same category.

Putnam's system is also used by other large libraries. However, many school libraries and smaller public libraries use the Dewey Decimal System, which organizes books into 10 main categories identified by number.

Under Putnam's direction, the Library of Congress also introduced interlibrary loans—the practice of one library borrowing books from another library. Through interlibrary loan, the Library of Congress was opened up to all Americans. Putnam was questioned about the risk of books being lost or damaged when sent out of the library. But he believed that "a book used, is after all, fulfilling a

Putnam watched students in the reading room in 1899. Putnam helped students from all over the country gain access to the collection through interlibrary loan.

higher mission than a book which is merely being preserved for possible future use."

In 1931, the library launched a program to create books and other materials for blind and physically handi-capped readers. At the top of the list of tasks was choosing

27

15 books to be reproduced in Braille for a program test group. The first book ordered was a biography of George Washington by Woodrow Wilson, chosen because the country would celebrate the bicentennial of Washington's birth in 1932. With a selection of Braille books in place, the library then created a network of 18 libraries that would be able to serve handicapped readers throughout the country.

Finally, Putnam oversaw the construction of a second Library of Congress building, opened in 1939. The simple, rectangular building is now called the John Adams Building, after the second president of the

The Library of Congress filled a reading room with books and magazines in Braille for people who were blind.

United States. It provided more storage for the ever-growing collection.

In all, Putnam served as librarian of Congress for 40 years before retiring in 1939. President Franklin Roosevelt told Putnam, "Under your direction, our national library has become one of the great libraries of the world."

The John Adams Building was originally called the Annex.

THE LIBRARY AT WORK

The Library of Congress has continued to grow. Every day, it adds about 10,000 new books and other items to its collection. To keep pace, the library has expanded and updated its operations.

President James Madison

In 1965, Congress authorized the construction of a third library building in Washington. Dedicated in 1981, it was named the James Madison Memorial Building. It is the largest library building in the world.

Beginning in 1986, the Thomas Jefferson Building was restored. The project cost around $70 million, much more than what it cost to build the original structure. In the restoration, the main hallway's murals and mosaics were carefully cleaned and brought back to their original brilliance. The building was also modernized, complete with Internet access in the main reading room. After more than a decade of work, it was reopened in time for the library's bicentennial in 2000.

The restoration of the Thomas Jefferson Building was carefully researched so that the finished results matched the original building.

Unlike at most libraries, visitors to the Library of Congress may not browse through the bookshelves or check materials out. Patrons must request a specific item. A librarian will locate the item and bring it to the patron, who can use it inside the library. Only visitors over high school age can use the library's collections.

What will researchers find at the Library of Congress? They can listen to recordings of American Indian music and traditional American music, like blues and folk. They can study the same hand-drawn maps used by explorers of the 1400s. They can read original manuscripts of works by Walt Whitman and other famous poets and authors. Or they can take a look at the world's largest collection of films and television programs.

One of the most popular sections of the library is the local history and genealogy collection. It allows people to research their family history and create family trees. The library's genealogy collection is one of the world's most complete. Visitors use everything from old military service records to phone directories from more than 120,000 American cities and towns to help build their knowledge of their family's past.

Researchers at the library can dig into a vast collection of rare and unusual objects that help bring history alive. The library owns the objects found in Abraham Lincoln's pockets the night he was assassinated. They include his eyeglasses, a pocketknife, and a clipping from a newspaper. The library is also home to Thomas Jefferson's

Many visitors ask to see the objects President Lincoln had in his pockets the night he was shot.

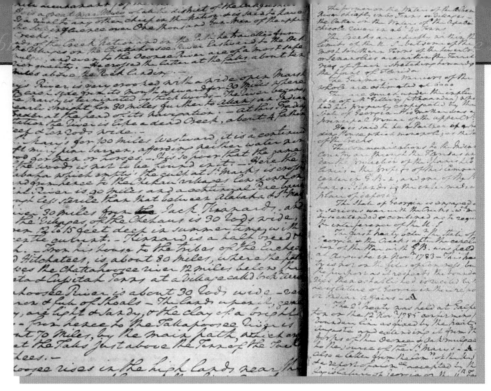

A handwritten memo by President George Washington is kept in the Library of Congress.

original draft of the Declaration of Independence. Visible on the margins are the scribbled changes suggested by Benjamin Franklin. And then there are the notebooks of inventor Alexander Graham Bell, which include his first drawings of the telephone.

The library's collection includes material from all over the world. In fact, about half of the Library of Congress' books are in languages other than English. In all, the library offers books in 460 languages. The Asian Division of the library alone has 2 million items from

China, Japan, and Korea. To help collect more international material, the Library of Congress maintains offices in other countries.

The library is known for the many rare and unusual books it owns. The smallest of its books is called *Old King Cole*, which measures just ½ inch (1.3 centimeters) wide and ½ inch tall. One of its best-known books is called the

A student in the 1940s reads from a book about ancient China in the Asian Division. The division was started in 1869 with 933 volumes from the emperor of China.

Giant Bible of Mainz. This 500-year-old hand-lettered book is prized for its beauty. The Library of Congress also owns a copy of the Gutenberg Bible, which was produced on the world's first printing press to use moveable metal type in Germany in 1453.

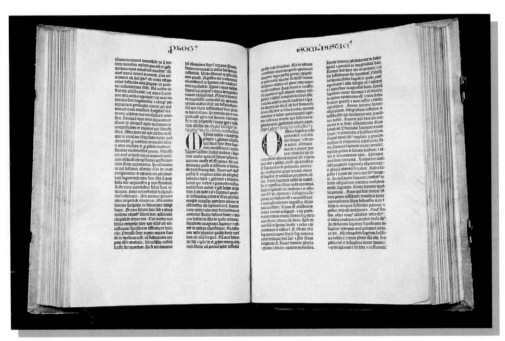

The Gutenberg Bible is also known as the 42-line Bible or the Mazarin Bible.

THE LIBRARY AND THE FUTURE

Technology has changed the way all libraries work, and the Library of Congress is no exception. Today, library users can access computer databases to find the information they are seeking.

But long before computers were introduced, the Library of Congress developed a system that used index

A woman sorts through the card catalog in the mid-1900s. The card catalog is now computerized, but visitors can still use the drawers to find books that were cataloged prior to 1980.

cards to keep track of books. One card was created for each of the library's books or other materials. That card was kept in alphabetical order in a card catalog. The system was adopted by libraries throughout the nation and the world.

The Library of Congress' catalog has been computerized since 1981. Technology has made it possible for patrons to find information more quickly and easily than ever. Technology also makes it possible to use the library without even leaving home.

The American Memory National Digital Library offers access to more than 8 million historical items on the Internet. Researchers all over the world can look at photographs from the Civil War, read historic political cartoons, and watch early movies right on their computer screens.

Technology also promises to help solve one of the great problems facing the Library of Congress and all libraries. Books fall apart over time. For the last 150 years or so, most books have been printed on paper made from

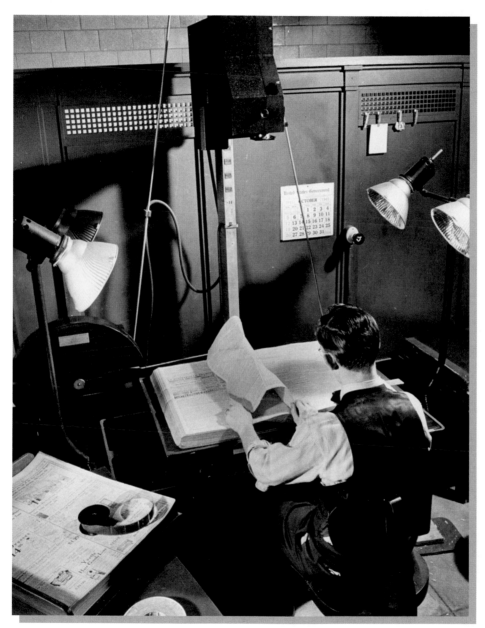

A Library of Congress employee checks microfilm for quality in the 1940s.

wood pulp. The acids in this paper cause the pages to slowly decay and eventually fall apart. Librarians are racing against time to preserve the contents of books before they are no longer usable. The Library of Congress has put the contents of many books on microfilm. Other books are being transferred to computer disks that can hold as much

Librarian of Congress James H. Billington

as 20,000 pages of information.

The Library of Congress began as a collection of books and maps sent across the ocean from England to the United States. Today, it includes technological wonders that could not have been imagined in 1800. People all over the globe can use the library's materials simply by clicking on their computer's mouse.

James H. Billington, who became the 13th librarian of Congress in 1987, has said that the Library of Congress aims to "increase the knowledge available to Americans in their local communities." The Library of Congress is no longer just Congress' library. It has become a library for all the people of the United States and the world beyond.

GLOSSARY

access—to enter and make use of something

assassinated—to have murdered someone well known or important

fireproof—not easily burned

joint committee—a group made up of members of the Senate and the House of Representatives

microfilm—a film that carries very small photographs of printed material

patrons—people who use a library or other facility

pocketknife—a knife that folds up and can be carried in a pocket

restoration—the act of bringing something back to its former condition

tablets—flat slabs of clay or other solid material into which words can be carved

volumes—books

DID YOU KNOW?

- The Library of Congress receives about 22,000 items every day. Of these, the library keeps about 10,000 for its collection. The remaining items are passed on to other libraries or schools.

- During the Civil War, President Abraham Lincoln borrowed a book on military science from the library. He kept it for two years. There is no record of any overdue charge.

- Each year, the librarian of Congress names the national poet laureate. The poet laureate works from the Library of Congress to encourage the appreciation of poetry.

IMPORTANT DATES

Timeline

1800	President John Adams approves an act of Congress that establishes the Library of Congress.
1814	British troops burn the U.S. Capitol and destroy the Library of Congress.
1815	Congress approves the purchase of Thomas Jefferson's book collection to replace the burned Library of Congress collection.
1851	Another fire greatly damages the library's collection.
1853	Library of Congress reopens in a new fire proof room in the Capitol.
1897	New Library of Congress building (now called the Thomas Jefferson Building) opens.
1939	Second Library of Congress building, the John Adams Building, opens.
1981	Third Library of Congress building, the James Madison Building, opens.
2000	Library of Congress celebrates 200th anniversary of its establishment.

IMPORTANT PEOPLE

JOHN JAMES BECKLEY (1757–1807)

First librarian of Congress who served from 1802 to 1807

THOMAS JEFFERSON (1743–1826)

Third president of the United States, author of the Declaration of Independence, and early supporter of the Library of Congress

HERBERT PUTNAM (1861–1955)

Librarian of Congress from 1899 to 1939 who established the Library of Congress Classification System

AINSWORTH RAND SPOFFORD (1825–1908)

Librarian of Congress from 1864 to 1897 who helped turn the library into a national institution

GEORGE WATTERSTON (1783–1854)

Librarian of Congress from 1815 to 1829 who helped rebuild the library after British troops set fire to the U.S. Capitol and destroyed the library collection

WANT TO KNOW MORE?

At the Library

Fowler, Allan. *The Library of Congress*. New York: Children's Press, 1996.

The Library of Congress: An Architectural Alphabet. San Francisco: Pomegranate, in association with the Library of Congress, 2000.

Raatma, Lucia. *Libraries*. New York: Children's Press, 1998.

Sakurai, Gail. *The Library of Congress*. New York: Scholastic, 1999.

On the Web

For more information on the *Library of Congress*, use FactHound to track down Web sites related to this book.

1. Go to *www.facthound.com*

2. Type in a search word related to this book or this book ID: 0756516315

3. Click on the *Fetch It* button.

Your trusty FactHound will fetch the best Web sites for you!

On the Road

The Library of Congress

101 Independence Ave., S.E.

Washington, DC 20540

202/ 707-8000

www.loc.gov

Visit the three buildings of the Library of Congress

Look for more We the People books about this era:

The Alamo
ISBN 0-7565-0097-4

The Arapaho and Their History
ISBN 0-7565-0831-2

The Battle of the Little Bighorn
ISBN 0-7565-0150-4

The Buffalo Soldiers
ISBN 0-7565-0833-9

The California Gold Rush
ISBN 0-7565-0041-9

California Ranchos
ISBN 0-7565-1633-1

The Cherokee and Their History
ISBN 0-7565-1273-5

The Chumash and Their History
ISBN 0-7565-0835-5

The Creek and Their History
ISBN 0-7565-0836-3

The Erie Canal
ISBN 0-7565-0679-4

Great Women of Pioneer America
ISBN 0-7565-1269-7

Great Women of the Old West
ISBN 0-7565-0099-0

The Iroquois and Their History
ISBN 0-7565-1272-7

The Klondike Gold Rush
ISBN 0-7565-1630-7

The Lewis and Clark Expedition
ISBN 0-7565-0044-3

The Louisiana Purchase
ISBN 0-7565-0210-1

The Mexican War
ISBN 0-7565-0841-X

The Ojibwe and Their History
ISBN 0-7565-0843-6

The Oregon Trail
ISBN 0-7565-0045-1

The Pony Express
ISBN 0-7565-0301-9

The Powhatan and Their History
ISBN 0-7565-0844-4

The Pueblo and Their History
ISBN 0-7565-1274-3

The Santa Fe Trail
ISBN 0-7565-0047-8

The Sioux and Their History
ISBN 0-7565-1275-1

The Trail of Tears
ISBN 0-7565-0101-6

The Transcontinental Railroad
ISBN 0-7565-0153-9

The Wampanoag and Their History
ISBN 0-7565-0847-9

The War of 1812
ISBN 0-7565-0848-7

The Wilderness Road
ISBN 0-7565-1637-4

A complete list of We the People titles is available on our Web site:
www.compasspointbooks.com

INDEX

About the Author

Andrew Santella writes for magazines and newspapers, including *GQ* and the *New York Times Book Review*. He is the author of a number of books for young readers. He lives outside Chicago with his wife and son.